start it

start it

It's not what you've got, it's what you do with IT

APPLE

A QUINTET BOOK

Published by The Apple Press
6 Blundell Street
London N7 9BH

ISBN 1-84092-145-5

This book was designed and produced by
Quintet Publishing Limited
6 Blundell Street
London N7 9BH

Creative Director: Rebecca Martin
Designer: Deep Creative, London
Project Editor: Debbie Foy
Series Editor: Deborah Gray

Typeset in Great Britain by
Central Southern Typesetters, Eastbourne
Manufactured in Malaysia by CH Colour Scan
Printed in China by Leefung-Asco Printers Ltd.

Material in this book has previously appeared in other Quintet titles.

> **Because of the slight risk of salmonella, raw
> eggs should not be served to the very young,
> the ill or the elderly, or to pregnant women.**

contents

Introduction   6

Dunk it   Soups & Breads   7

Dip it   Dips, Salsas & Pâtés   19

Savour it   Vegetables   33

Sample it   Fish & Seafood   57

Anticipate it   Meat & Poultry   71

Index   80

introduction

A starter should be a feast for the eyes and a flavourful ff
main event to come. This appetizing book is brimful of ex
that will leave your guests breathless with anticipation, s
for the meal and ensuring that it kicks off in style.

Avoid spending hours on meticulous preparation, followin
of straightforward recipes, complemented by clear, step
instructions and tantalizing illustrations. No compromise
when it comes to taste, as all the dishes are tempting a
some traditional and some with a twist!

Ladle up an appetizing soup. Dressed up or down, serve
dramatic bread and soup combo is always an impressiv
Or dip into dips, salsas and pâtés – a perfect recipe for
course. Savour a vegetarian starter to suit all palates, f
Stuffed Peppers to the new and notable, with a range o
influences, such as Onion and Green Pepper Pie from t

Sample a fresh fish opener, from an exciting array of k
glamorous Giant Prawn Gratin. Whatever you decide o
down a storm because these recipes work from three
fresh ingredients, simple preparation and thoughtful se

With these starters you'll always know where to begin

dunk it

soups & breads

roasted pumpkin and smoked mussel soup

Ingredients

SERVES 6

1/2 SMALL PUMPKIN OR
1 MEDIUM FIRM-FLESHED
SQUASH (ABOUT 450 G/1 LB)

FRESHLY GROUND
BLACK PEPPER

3 TBSP OLIVE OIL

1 LEEK, FINELY SLICED

2 STICKS CELERY,
TRIMMED AND SLICED

1 CARROT, SLICED

2 TSP GROUND CORIANDER

3-4 SPRIGS FRESH THYME

1 BAY LEAF

750 ML/1 1/4 PT WELL-
FLAVOURED VEGETABLE STOCK

450 ML/3/4 PT MILK

175 G/6 OZ SMOKED
MUSSELS

SALT

PARSLEY, FRESHLY CHOPPED

Preheat oven to 220°C/425°F/Gas Mark 7. Cut pumpkin into slices about 5 cm/2 in wide and place them in a roasting tin. You will need six slices. Season lightly with pepper then brush flesh with olive oil. Bake in oven for about 30 minutes, until pumpkin is tender. Scoop flesh from skin and place to one side.

Heat 2 tablespoons of olive oil in a large pan; add leek, celery and carrot and cook slowly until soft. Stir in ground coriander and cook slowly for a further minute. Add pumpkin flesh to pan with thyme and bay leaf, then pour in stock. Bring to the boil then cover and simmer for 35 to 40 minutes.

Allow soup to cool slightly then purée until smooth in a blender. Rinse pan then return soup to it with milk and bring slowly to simmering point. Add smoked mussels, season well with salt and pepper and heat for another minute or two. Garnish with chopped parsley just before serving.

beer mustard bread

Ingredients

MAKES 1 LOAF

**1 PACKAGE (2¹/₄ TSP)
ACTIVE DRY YEAST**

1¹/₂ TBSP SUGAR

**1¹/₄ CUPS WARM FLAT BEER,
40-45°C/105-115°F**

3 TBSP POWDERED MILK

1¹/₂ TBSP VEGETABLE OIL

3 TBSP DIJON MUSTARD

³/₄ TSP DRIED THYME

1¹/₂ TSP SALT

**ABOUT 350 G/12 OZ STRONG WHITE
OR PLAIN FLOUR**

Dissolve active dry yeast and sugar in warm beer. Let yeast build up a foamy head, approximately 5 to 10 minutes.

Mix all remaining ingredients except flour. Put about 300 g/10 oz flour into a large bowl and stir in oil mixture. When yeast is ready, stir it into flour. Turn dough out onto a floured surface. Knead with floured hands, adding flour as needed, for about 10 minutes, until you have a smooth dough that is neither sticky nor overly stiff. Place dough in a greased bowl and turn it over so all surfaces are lightly oiled. Loosely cover bowl and leave it in a warm place to rise until it has doubled in bulk, about 1¹/₂ hours.

Knock back and knead it lightly. Let it rest while you grease a 23-cm/9-in loaf tin. Gently shape dough into a loaf and put it in pan. Put pan in a warm place and loosely cover it. Let it rise until doubled in volume, about 1 hour. Twenty minutes before dough has finished rising, preheat oven to 180°C/350°F/Gas Mark 4. Put loaf in oven and bake until golden, 25 to 30 minutes.

crisp breadsticks

Ingredients

MAKES 36 BREADSTICKS

1 PACKAGE (2¹/₄ TSP) ACTIVE
DRY YEAST

1 TBSP SUGAR

1 CUP WARM WATER,
40–45°C/105–115°F

ABOUT 350 G/12 OZ STRONG WHITE
OR PLAIN FLOUR

6 TBSP VEGETABLE OIL

1¹/₂ TSP SALT

ABOUT 3 TBSP VEGETABLE OIL

1 EGG WHITE

2 TBSP WATER

SESAME OR POPPY SEEDS
OR COARSE SALT, (OPTIONAL)

Dissolve active dry yeast and sugar in warm water. Let yeast build up a
foamy head, approximately 5 to 10 minutes.

Put about 300 g/10 oz flour in a large bowl. Mix in 6 tablespoons oil and
salt. When yeast is ready, stir it into flour. Turn dough out onto a floured
surface. Knead with floured hands, adding flour as needed, for about
10 minutes, until you have a smooth dough that is neither sticky nor
overly stiff. Place dough in a greased bowl and turn it over so all surfaces
are lightly oiled. Loosely cover bowl and leave it in a warm place to rise
until doubled in bulk, about 1¹/₂ hours.

Grease two or three baking sheets. When dough is ready, knock back and
knead lightly. Cut into 36 pieces. Roll each piece between your palms to
form a very skinny rope, about 20 cm/8 in long. Place breadsticks widely
spaced apart on baking sheets. Brush lightly with oil. Cover loosely and
set in a warm place to rise, 20 to 25 minutes.

Preheat oven to 180°C/350°F/Gas Mark 4. Make wash of egg white and
2 tablespoons water. Brush egg wash lightly over breadsticks. Sprinkle
with seeds or salt, if desired. Bake until golden brown, about 25 minutes.

seafood chowder

Ingredients

SERVES 4

2 TBSP OLIVE OIL

2 LEEKS, SLICED

1 SMALL ONION, THINLY SLICED

1 CARROT, DICED

1 CELERY STALK, DICED

1 POTATO, DICED

600 ML/1 PT FISH STOCK

1 BOUQUET GARNI

450 G/1 LB COD FILLET, SKINNED

600 ML/1 PT MILK

8 SCALLOPS, SHELLED

100 G/4 OZ QUICK-COOK MACARONI

SALT AND BLACK PEPPER

350 G/12 OZ COOKED MUSSELS

350 G/12 OZ PEELED, COOKED PRAWNS

4 TBSP PARSLEY, CHOPPED

FRESHLY GRATED PARMESAN CHEESE,

Heat oil in a large saucepan. Add leeks, onion, carrot, celery and potato. Cook, stirring well, until leeks have reduced, and onion has softened slightly but not browned. Pour in stock and bring to the boil. Add bouquet garni, reduce heat, and cover pan. Simmer for 20 minutes.

Meanwhile, put cod in a saucepan, and add milk. Heat gently until milk is just about to simmer, then poach fish for 2 to 3 minutes, until just cooked. Remove fish from milk, and set it aside on a plate. Poach scallops in milk for 2 to 3 minutes, until just cooked. Set milk aside.

Flake cod, discarding any bones, and slice scallops. Add macaroni and salt and pepper to soup, and bring back to the boil. Then reduce heat, cover, and cook for about 7 minutes, or until macaroni is just tender. Pour in poaching milk, and heat, stirring all the time.

Taste soup for seasoning; then add cooked cod, scallops, mussels and prawns. Gently stir in parsley, and heat for 2 to 3 minutes, or until seafood is hot. Serve at once, with freshly grated Parmesan cheese.

tomato-basil soup

Ingredients

SERVES 4

2 CLOVES GARLIC, FINELY CHOPPED

5 TBSP FRESH BASIL, CHOPPED

1/4 TSP FRESHLY GROUND
BLACK PEPPER

3 TBSP EXTRA-VIRGIN OLIVE OIL

2 KG/4 LB RIPE TOMATOES

200 ML/8 FL OZ CHICKEN STOCK

1 TBSP BALSAMIC VINEGAR

1/2 TSP SALT

8 TBSP SWEET RED PEPPER OR
TOMATO SALSA

In a small bowl, mix together garlic, 1 tablespoon basil, black pepper and olive oil. Lightly crush garlic with the back of a spoon to release the juices into the oil. Let mixture steep while you prepare the tomatoes.

Peel tomatoes by dropping them into a pot of boiling water for about 40 seconds. Let them cool slightly, then slip off skins. Cut them in half and squeeze out seeds. Core and coarsely chop tomatoes.

Put tomatoes, chicken stock and garlic-oil mixture into a medium saucepan. Bring to the boil, then reduce heat to low and simmer, uncovered, 1 hour. Add remaining basil, balsamic vinegar and salt, then purée the soup. Taste and adjust seasonings. Chill until serving time. Top with a spoonful of sweet red pepper or tomato salsa, stirred into the soup.

bagels

Ingredients

MAKES 12 TO 15 BAGELS

1 PACKAGE (2¼ TSP)
ACTIVE DRY YEAST

1 TBSP SUGAR

200 ML/8 FL OZ WARM MILK,
40–45°C/105–115°F

350 G/12 OZ STRONG WHITE FLOUR

1 EGG

1½ TBSP VEGETABLE OIL

¾ TSP SALT

1 TBSP SUGAR

GLAZE

1 EGG WHITE

2 TSP WATER

SESAME OR POPPY SEEDS

Dissolve dry yeast and 1 tablespoon sugar in warm milk. Let yeast build up a foamy head, approximately 5 to 10 minutes.

Put about 300 g/12 oz flour in a large bowl. Mix in egg, oil and salt. When yeast is ready, stir it into flour. Turn dough out onto a floured surface. Knead, adding flour, for about 10 minutes, until you have a smooth dough that is neither sticky nor overly stiff. Place dough in a greased bowl and turn it over so all surfaces are lightly oiled. Loosely cover the bowl and leave it in a warm place to rise until doubled in bulk, about 1½ hours.

Knock back dough and cut into 12 to 15 pieces. Roll each piece between your palms to form a thin rope, about 20 cm/8 in long with tapered ends. Bring ends together to form a circle, with ends overlapping. With moistened fingers, pinch or lightly knead joined ends so the circle is securely fastened, or it will come apart later.

Set the bagels in a warm place to rise for 15 minutes and cover loosely. Preheat oven to 200°C/400°F/Gas Mark 6. While they are rising, bring a large saucepan of water to the boil. Add 1 tablespoon sugar. Drop the bagels one or two at a time into boiling water, handling them as gently as possible so they do not deflate. They will rise to the surface of the water and swell up. Let them cook 1 minute, then turn and cook 3 minutes more.

Remove bagels, let drain over the water and place on a ungreased baking sheet. Beat egg white with water and brush over bagels. Sprinkle with sesame or poppy seeds. Bake until golden, 20 to 25 minutes.

rye crescent rolls

Ingredients

MAKES **24** ROLLS

1 PACKAGE (**2**¹⁄₄ TSP) ACTIVE DRY YEAST

1¹⁄₂ TBSP HONEY

200 ML/**8** OZ WARM FLAT BEER, **40-45**°C/**105-115**°F

3 TBSP VEGETABLE OIL

1¹⁄₂ TSP SALT

1¹⁄₂ TSP CARAWAY SEEDS

100 G/**4** OZ RYE FLOUR

ABOUT **275** G/**10** OZ STRONG WHITE OR PLAIN FLOUR

3 TBSP MELTED BUTTER

Dissolve active dry yeast and honey in the warm beer. Let yeast build up a foamy head, approximately 5 to 10 minutes.

Mix oil, salt, caraway seeds and rye flour. When yeast Is ready, stir it into rye flour mixture. Stir in white flour, 50 g/2 oz at a time. When the dough becomes too tough to stir, turn it out onto a floured surface. Knead, adding flour, for about 10 minutes, until you have a smooth dough that is neither sticky nor overly stiff. Place dough in a greased bowl and turn over so all surfaces are lightly oiled. Loosely cover bowl and leave in a warm place to rise until doubled in bulk, about 1¹⁄₂ hours.

Knock back dough and cut into three equal parts. Let dough rest for 5 minutes. Oil two or three baking sheets.

On a lightly floured surface, roll out first section of dough into a circle roughly 23 cm/9 in diameter. Cut circle into eight wedges. Starting from outside of circle and working towards the point, loosely roll up each wedge. Stretch each roll slightly and pull it into a curve. Set it on baking sheet with point underneath. Repeat with all wedges, then with remaining dough.

Let dough rise until doubled, about 1 hour. Brush rolls with melted butter. Bake in a preheated 200°C/400°F/Gas Mark 6 oven until lightly browned, about 12 to 15 minutes.

lebanese couscous soup

Ingredients

SERVES 6

4 LARGE ONIONS,
FINELY SLICED

3 CLOVES GARLIC,
FINELY SLICED

2 TBSP VEGETABLE OIL

12 G/$^1/_2$ OZ BUTTER

1 RED CHILLI, SEEDED
AND FINELY CHOPPED

1 TSP MILD CHILLI POWDER

$^1/_2$ TSP GROUND TURMERIC

1 TSP GROUND CORIANDER

SALT AND FRESHLY
GROUND BLACK PEPPER

2 L/3$^1/_2$ PT WELL-FLAVOURED
VEGETABLE OR CHICKEN STOCK

75 G/3 OZ COUSCOUS

FRESHLY CHOPPED CORIANDER,
TO GARNISH

Cook onions and garlic in the oil and butter until well browned, about 15 minutes, over a medium-high heat. Let onions brown to achieve a rich colour for the finished soup.

Stir in chopped chilli and spices and cook over a low heat for a further 1 to 2 minutes before adding stock. Season lightly then bring to the boil. Cover and simmer for 30 minutes.

Stir couscous into soup, return to the boil, and simmer for a further 10 minutes. Season to taste then garnish with coriander and serve immediately.

thai spiced chicken soup

Ingredients

SERVES 4

1-2 TBSP PEANUT OR
SUNFLOWER OIL

2 SMALL, BONELESS CHICKEN
BREASTS, SKINNED AND
SHREDDED

2 TBSP THAI 7-SPICE
SEASONING

1 STICK LEMON GRASS,
FINELY CHOPPED

2 MEDIUM POTATOES, DICED

750 ML/1¼ PT CHICKEN OR
VEGETABLE STOCK

450 ML/¾ PT MILK

3-4 SPRING ONIONS, TRIMMED
AND FINELY SLICED

100 G/4 OZ FROZEN PEAS

1-2 TBSP SATAY SAUCE
OR PEANUT BUTTER

SALT AND FRESHLY GROUND
BLACK PEPPER

1-2 TBSP DOUBLE CREAM,
TO GARNISH

Heat oil in a large pan; add chicken and 7-spice seasoning and cook quickly until chicken begins to brown. Stir in lemon grass and potato, then add liquids. Bring slowly to the boil, then cover and simmer for 20 minutes.

Stir spring onions into soup with peas; return to the boil, then continue cooking for a further 5 minutes.

Add satay sauce or peanut butter to soup just before serving. Remove from heat and stir until melted. Season to taste then serve, garnished with a spoonful of double cream.

crab and sweet corn soup

Ingredients

SERVES 6

425-G/15-OZ CAN SWEET CORN

225-G/8-OZ CAN WHITE CRABMEAT

1 L/1³/₄ PT WELL-FLAVOURED FISH OR VEGETABLE STOCK

SALT AND FRESHLY GROUND BLACK PEPPER

1 TBSP SOY SAUCE

2 EGG WHITES (SEE NOTE, P.4)

CHOPPED SPRING ONIONS

Bring sweet corn, crabmeat, stock, seasoning and soy sauce to the boil in a large pan, stirring to mix sweet corn and crab evenly throughout soup. Simmer for about 10 minutes.

Whisk egg whites into soft peaks, then stir carefully into soup just before serving. Garnish with a scattering of freshly chopped spring onions.

dip it

dips, salsas & pâtés

nut and cheese
pepper slices

Ingredients

SERVES 4

150 G/5 OZ MIXED SHELLED NUTS
(PEANUTS, CASHEWS,
ALMONDS, ETC)

SALT

CAYENNE PEPPER

225 G/8 OZ LOW FAT CREAM CHEESE

1 CLOVE GARLIC, FINELY CHOPPED

FRESHLY GROUND BLACK PEPPER

1 MEDIUM RED PEPPER

1 MEDIUM GREEN PEPPER

WHOLEMEAL TOAST

Heat a frying pan over a medium heat, then add nuts and cook until browned. Scatter some salt and cayenne over some kitchen paper, add hot nuts and toss in seasonings. Chop nuts roughly when cooled.

Beat cream cheese until smooth, then add garlic and nuts. Season to taste with extra salt and black pepper. Cut tops from peppers and remove seeds and cores. Pack filling into peppers, pressing down firmly with the back of a spoon until peppers are full.

Chill for 2 to 3 hours before slicing. Serve a slice each of red and green pepper, with wholemeal toast.

mushroom and
hazelnut pâté

Ingredients

SERVES 6 TO 8

225 G/8 OZ HAZELNUTS, TOASTED
AND ROUGHLY CHOPPED

65 G/2½ OZ FRESH WHOLEMEAL
BREADCRUMBS, TIGHTLY PACKED

1 MEDIUM ONION

2 PLUMP CLOVES GARLIC

450 G/1 LB MUSHROOMS, TRIMMED

50 G/2 OZ BUTTER

SALT AND FRESHLY
GROUND BLACK PEPPER

2 TBSP SOY SAUCE

1 LARGE EGG, BEATEN

2 THIN SLICES STREAKY BACON
(OPTIONAL)

Preheat oven to 180°C/350°F/Gas Mark 4. Combine hazelnuts with breadcrumbs and chop onion, garlic and mushrooms finely.

Melt butter in a large frying pan, add mushroom mixture, and cook slowly for about 5 minutes. Allow to cool slightly, then add to hazelnut mixture with plenty of salt, pepper and soy sauce. Blend together with beaten egg.

Lightly grease a small loaf tin. Stretch bacon with the back of a knife, then arrange it in base of tin. Spoon the hazelnut mixture into tin and smooth top. Cover with greased aluminium foil and place in a shallow roasting tin. Half fill roasting tin with hot water.

Bake in preheated oven for 1 hour, then remove pâté from roasting tin and allow to cool. Chill pâté overnight in refrigerator, then loosen it in tin with a flat knife. Serve on a bed of green salad.

hummus

Ingredients

SERVES 8

150 G/5 OZ CHICKPEAS, SOAKED OVERNIGHT

2-3 PLUMP CLOVES GARLIC

5 TBSP TAHINI (SESAME PASTE)

100 ML/4 FL OZ OLIVE OIL

SALT AND FRESHLY GROUND BLACK PEPPER

JUICE OF HALF A LEMON

PAPRIKA

Rinse chickpeas under cold running water, then bring to the boil in pan of fresh water and simmer for about 1½ hours, until tender. Leave to cool, then drain peas, reserving some of the water.

Place peas in a blender or food processor with garlic, tahini and olive oil and blend. Add as much water from the beans as necessary to make a thick paste. Season well with salt and pepper, then add lemon juice to taste.

Spoon the hummus into a serving dish and chill lightly. Sprinkle with paprika just before serving.

traditional guacamole

Ingredients

SERVES 4

2 LARGE RIPE AVOCADOS

2 TOMATOES, SEEDED AND CHOPPED

1 MILD GREEN CHILLI, SEEDED AND FINELY CHOPPED

GRATED ZEST AND JUICE OF 1 LIME

2 SPRING ONIONS, TRIMMED AND FINELY CHOPPED

1-2 GARLIC CLOVES, FINELY CHOPPED

$^1/_2$ TSP SALT

Scoop flesh from avocados and mash it roughly with a fork. Add all remaining ingredients, seasoning gradually with salt to taste. Serve with corn chips, tortilla chips or a selection of sliced vegetables.

aubergine guacamole

Ingredients

SERVES 4 TO 6

1 LARGE AUBERGINE

1 AVOCADO, PEELED
AND FINELY CHOPPED

JUICE AND ZEST OF 1 LIME

2 TOMATOES, SEEDED
AND FINELY CHOPPED

1 GREEN CHILLI, SEEDED
AND FINELY CHOPPED

1 TBSP ONION,
FINELY CHOPPED

1-2 GARLIC CLOVES,
FINELY CHOPPED

SALT AND FRESHLY
GROUND BLACK PEPPER

OLIVE OIL, TO DRIZZLE

PAPRIKA, TO TASTE

Preheat oven to 220°C/425°F/Gas Mark 7. Prick aubergine all over, place on a baking sheet, and roast for 30 to 40 minutes, until wrinkled and tender. Cover with a damp cloth and leave to cool completely, about 1 hour.

Peel aubergine, then chop into small pieces. Blend to a fairly smooth paste in a food processor, then turn into a small bowl. Toss avocado with lime juice and zest, then add to aubergine with next four ingredients. Stir carefully until well combined. Season generously with salt and pepper, then drizzle with a little olive oil and sprinkle with paprika.

Serve with tortilla chips or warm toast.

avocado salsa

Ingredients

SERVES 4

2 LARGE, RIPE AVOCADOS,
STONED AND DICED

3 TBSP FRESH LIME JUICE

1 TBSP OLIVE OIL

1 SMALL RED ONION,
FINELY CHOPPED

1/2 RED PEPPER, DICED

3 JALAPEÑO CHILLIES,
FINELY CHOPPED

1 LARGE SEEDED AND
CHOPPED TOMATO

1 TBSP FRESH CORIANDER,
CHOPPED

2 GARLIC CLOVES,
FINELY CHOPPED

SALT AND PEPPER, TO TASTE

Mix avocado chunks with lime juice and olive oil, then stir in remaining ingredients. Taste and adjust seasoning.

olive salsa

Ingredients

SERVES 4 TO 6

**200-G/7-OZ CAN OF
STONED GREEN OLIVES**

**75-G/3-OZ CAN OF
STONED BLACK OLIVES**

**3 GARLIC CLOVES,
FINELY CHOPPED**

**2 JALAPEÑO CHILES,
FINELY CHOPPED**

**1 SMALL RED ONION,
FINELY CHOPPED**

**1/2 SMALL RED PEPPER,
CHOPPED**

**50 G/2 OZ ANCHOVY FILLETS
(ABOUT 15), FINELY CHOPPED**

**25 G/1 OZ PINE NUTS, LIGHTLY
TOASTED**

2 TBSP OLIVE OIL

1 TBSP RED WINE VINEGAR

Drain olives and coarsely chop them. Mix with all remaining ingredients and let flavours blend for at least 30 minutes before serving.

To toast pine nuts: Preheat oven to 150°C/300°F/Gas Mark 3. Spread pine nuts in a single layer on a small baking sheet or a doubled sheet of aluminium foil. Bake for 5 to 10 minutes until they are lightly browned. Watch them closely, as they burn easily.

taramasalata

Ingredients

SERVES 4 TO 6

3 SLICES OF WHITE BREAD

100 G/4 OZ TARAMA (COD'S ROE USUALLY SOLD IN A JAR)

1 FRESHLY BOILED, TENDER, PEELED POTATO, LIGHTLY MASHED

1–2 GARLIC CLOVES, FINELY CHOPPED

1 SMALL ONION, CHOPPED

JUICE OF 2 LEMONS

175–225 ML/6–8 FL OZ EXTRA-VIRGIN OLIVE OIL

2–3 SPRING ONIONS, THINLY SLICED

SEVERAL SPRIGS OF FRESH DILL, CHOPPED

BLACK OLIVES, TO GARNISH

Soak bread in cold water for 1 minute, then squeeze it dry.

Place tarama, soaked bread, potato, garlic, onion and lemon juice in a blender, and beat until it forms a thick paste. Blend until smooth or slightly textured, as preferred.

Slowly add olive oil, a few tablespoons at a time, blending in between, until a thick, aromatic tarama-mayonnaise is formed. Taste and check for texture: if it is too strong, heavy or dense, blend in a few tablespoons of water. Remove from blender and stir in spring onions and chopped dill.

Spoon into a bowl and chill, then garnish with black olives and serve with fresh bread.

salmon pâté

Ingredients

SERVES 4

ONE **225-G/8-OZ** SALMON FILLET

100 G/4 OZ CREAM CHEESE

1 TBSP LIGHT SOY SAUCE

1 TBSP FRESH DILL, CHOPPED

1 TBSP FRESH PARSLEY, CHOPPED

1 TBSP LEMON JUICE

1 TBSP CAPERS

GROUND BLACK PEPPER

$^1/_2$ TSP PAPRIKA

DILL SPRIGS AND LEMON SLICES, TO GARNISH

HOT TOAST TRIANGLES

Poach salmon fillet in a large, shallow pan for 8 to 10 minutes or until cooked through. Remove from pan, drain and skin fish. Chop fish into pieces and leave to cool completely.

Place cream cheese, soy sauce, dill, parsley, lemon juice, capers, pepper and cooked salmon in a food processor, and blend for 15 seconds.

Transfer to four individual ramekins or small dishes. Sprinkle with paprika and chill until required. Garnish with dill and lemon, and serve with hot toast triangles.

andalusian salsa

Ingredients

SERVES 4

$^1/_2$ CUCUMBER, DICED

3-5 SMALL, RIPE TOMATOES, DICED

1 CARROT, DICED

1 RED PEPPER, DICED

1 GREEN PEPPER, DICED
(ADD A YELLOW OR ORANGE PEPPER
TOO, IF DESIRED)

3-5 SPRING ONIONS, THINLY SLICED,
OR 1 SMALL ONION, CHOPPED

3-5 GARLIC CLOVES,
FINELY CHOPPED

$^1/_4$ TSP GROUND CUMIN
OR CUMIN SEEDS

SALT, TO TASTE

JUICE OF 1 LEMON

1 TSP SHERRY VINEGAR
OR WHITE WINE VINEGAR

3 TBSP EXTRA-VIRGIN
OLIVE OIL OR TO TASTE

2 TBSP FRESH HERBS, CHOPPED
(PARSLEY, CORIANDER, MARJORAM
AND/OR OREGANO)

Combine cucumber, tomatoes, carrot, red and green peppers, spring onions and garlic. Toss with cumin, salt, lemon, sherry or white wine vinegar, olive oil and herbs. Taste for seasoning, and chill until ready to eat. Serve with tortilla chips or fresh bread.

homemade tortilla chips

Ingredients

SERVES 4 TO 6

12 STALE TORTILLAS

100 G/4 OZ SALT (OPTIONAL)

450 ML/³/₄ PT WATER

VEGETABLE OIL FOR FRYING

Cut stale tortillas into strips or wedges. For salted chips, make a brine by dissolving salt in the water. Dip tortilla pieces into brine, then shake off excess water.

Pour 1 cm/½ in of vegetable oil into a deep frying pan and heat until oil is hot but not smoking. Add chips. If they are wet with brine, take care because oil will splatter. Cook chips until golden, turning once or twice, about 3 minutes, depending on heat of oil. Remove chips from oil, holding them briefly over pan to drain, then place them on kitchen paper. Give oil a few moments to reheat, then add a new batch of chips.

A fat-free alternative is to bake the chips. Preheat oven to 160°C/325°F/ Gas Mark 3. Spread prepared tortillas on an ungreased baking sheet. Bake, turning occasionally, until crisp and lightly browned, about 40 minutes.

black olive tapenade

Ingredients

MAKES **225** ML/**8** FL OZ

75 G/**3** OZ STONED BLACK
OLIVES

75 G/**3** OZ STONED KALAMATA
OR SPANISH GREEN OLIVES

6 ANCHOVIES

1 GARLIC CLOVE

3 TBSP CAPERS

12 G/$^1/_2$ OZ SUNDRIED
TOMATOES

4 TBSP FRESH BASIL, CHOPPED

1 TBSP FRESH THYME,
CHOPPED OR $^1/_4$ TSP DRIED

$^1/_4$ TSP BLACK PEPPER

2 TSP FRESH LEMON JUICE

2-3 TBSP OLIVE OIL

Combine all ingredients in a blender
or food processor. Process until well
chopped, but stop before mixture
turns into a smooth paste. Add a little
extra olive oil if mixture is too dry.

savour it

vegetables

roasted tomato
tartlets

Ingredients

SERVES 6

DOUGH

225 G/8 OZ FINE WHOLEMEAL FLOUR

40 G/$\frac{1}{2}$ OZ SESAME SEEDS

$\frac{1}{2}$ TSP SALT

1 LARGE EGG, BEATEN

5 TBSP OLIVE OIL

3-4 TBSP WATER

TOMATO FILLING

3 ONIONS, FINELY SLICED

2 GARLIC CLOVES, HALVED

3 TBSP FRUITY OLIVE OIL

3-4 SPRIGS FRESH THYME

2 BAY LEAVES

SALT AND FRESHLY GROUND BLACK PEPPER

4-5 LARGE TOMATOES, SLICED

Mix together flour, sesame seeds and salt, then make a well in the centre. Add egg and olive oil and mix to a soft dough, adding water as necessary. Divide mixture into six and shape to line six 10-cm/4-in individual tart dishes—this is more of a dough than a pastry and is easiest to mould into shape with your fingers. Chill tart shells for at least 30 minutes whilst preparing tartlet filling.

Cook onions and garlic in olive oil with thyme and bay leaves for 30 to 40 minutes, until well softened and reduced. Season to taste, then remove herbs from pan.

Preheat oven to 225°C/425°F/Gas Mark 7. Fill tart shells with onion mixture then top with tomatoes, overlapping the slices and brushing them lightly with olive oil. Season well with salt and pepper, then bake in preheated oven for 20 to 25 minutes, until dough is crisp and tomatoes are just starting to blacken. Serve hot or cold with a crisp, green leaf salad on the side.

ntakos (cretan sandwich)

Ingredients

SERVES 4

4 PAXIMADIA OR OTHER
WHOLEWHEAT CRACKERS

12 OR MORE RIPE, SWEET,
JUICY TOMATOES

SPRINKLE OF OREGANO

3 DOZEN BLACK GREEK OR
OTHER MEDITERRANEAN OLIVES,
STONED AND CUT INTO PIECES

225 G/**8** OZ OR SO
KEFALOTIRI OR PECORINO
CHEESE, THINLY SLICED
OR SHAVED

50-100 ML/**2-4** FL OZ OLIVE
OIL (PREFERABLY GREEK),
OR AS NEEDED

Arrange paximadia on a platter or on plates. Layer with tomatoes, oregano, olives and cheese, and drizzle generously with olive oil.

Leave to marinate for at least 4 hours at room temperature, then serve.

aubergine toasts

Ingredients

SERVES 4

AUBERGINE PASTE

225 G/8 OZ AUBERGINE, PEELED AND FINELY CHOPPED

1 EGG WHITE, LIGHTLY WHISKED

2 TSP SHERRY

2 TSP OYSTER SAUCE

PINCH OF GROUND GINGER

2 TSP CORNFLOUR

PINCH OF SALT

TOASTS

4 SLICES WHITE BREAD, CRUSTS REMOVED

VEGETABLE OIL FOR DEEP-FRYING

CHILLIES, THINLY SLICED, TO GARNISH

CUCUMBER, CHOPPED FINELY, TO GARNISH

Mix aubergine with remaining paste ingredients. Cut bread into bite-sized triangles, then spread on one side with aubergine paste.

Heat oil to 160°C/320°F in a wok, then carefully add triangles in batches with a spoon, paste side down, and fry for about 2 to 3 minutes, until bread is golden brown. Remove with a slotted spoon and drain on kitchen paper. Keep warm in a low oven until all the toasts are cooked.

Serve warm, garnished with sliced chillies and finely chopped cucumber

tortilla wheels with pineapple salsa

Ingredients

SERVES 6 TO 8

FILLING

75 G/3 OZ CREAM CHEESE

1 GREEN CHILLI, SEEDED AND FINELY CHOPPED

2 TBSP CORIANDER, FRESHLY CHOPPED

4 TOMATOES, SEEDED AND FINELY CHOPPED

4 SPRING ONIONS, FINELY CHOPPED

1 PEPPER, RED OR YELLOW, SEEDED AND FINELY CHOPPED

100 G/4 OZ CHEDDAR CHEESE, GRATED

SALT AND FRESHLY GROUND BLACK PEPPER

8 FLOUR TORTILLAS

SALSA

1 TBSP BLACK MUSTARD SEEDS

1 ORANGE

4 THICK SLICES PINEAPPLE, FRESH OR CANNED, CHOPPED

1 SMALL RED ONION, FINELY CHOPPED

1 SMALL GREEN CHILLI, SEEDED AND FINELY CHOPPED

2 TOMATOES, DICED

Beat cream cheese until smooth, then add all other ingredients for filling. Mix well and season to taste with salt and pepper. Divide mixture between tortillas, spreading it evenly. Place each tortilla on top of another, making four stacks of two, then roll them up tightly. Cover in cling film and chill for at least 2 hours.

Prepare salsa whilst tortilla rolls are chilling. Heat a nonstick frying pan until evenly hot, then add mustard seeds and cook for 1 to 2 minutes, until the seeds begin to pop. Allow to cool. Grate zest from orange, then peel it and chop flesh. Mix orange with mustard seeds and all other ingredients, seasoning to taste with salt and pepper. Allow salsa to stand until required for flavours to blend.

Preheat oven to 200°C/400°F/Gas Mark 6. Unwrap tortillas and trim away ends, then cut each roll into eight slices. Place on baking sheets and bake in preheated oven for 15 to 20 minutes, until well browned. Serve with pineapple salsa.

crostini

Ingredients

MAKES ABOUT 40 PIECES

1 LARGE RED PEPPER

2 BAGUETTES FRENCH BREAD, EACH CUT INTO ABOUT 20 SLICES

1 LARGE OR 2 SMALL TOMATOES, PEELED, SEEDED AND CHOPPED

3 GARLIC CLOVES, FINELY CHOPPED

75-G/3-OZ CAN OF BLACK OLIVES, DRAINED AND COARSELY CHOPPED

1 JALAPEÑO CHILLI, SEEDS INCLUDED, FINELY CHOPPED

ABOUT 8 ANCHOVY FILLETS, FINELY CHOPPED

2 TBSP FRESH BASIL, CHOPPED

1/4 TSP DRIED OREGANO

2 TBSP OLIVE OIL

SALT, TO TASTE

300–350 G/10–12 OZ FRESH MOZZARELLA, THINLY SLICED

Preheat grill. Rinse pepper, cut into four fairly flat pieces, and trim seeds and ribs. Place pieces under grill, skin side up. Grill until skin is blistered and mostly black. Remove peppers from the grill and place in a covered bowl to steam for 10 minutes.

Put bread on grill pan and grill, turning once, until golden on both sides. Meanwhile, peel and chop pepper. Put pepper in a bowl with tomatoes, garlic, olives, jalapeño, anchovy, basil, oregano and olive oil. Mix ingredients. Taste and season if necessary. This salsa improves after flavours have been allowed to blend for several hours.

Spoon a little tomato mixture on each slice of bread, avoiding watery juices that will have collected in salsa. Top with a thin slice of mozzarella cheese. Grill until cheese has bubbled. Serve immediately.

pasta baskets with vegetables

Ingredients

SERVES 4

100 G/4 OZ DRIED VERMICELLI

DASH OF OLIVE OIL

VEGETABLE OIL, FOR DEEP-FRYING

FILLING

2 TBSP SESAME OIL

2 OLOVES OF GARLIC,
FINELY CHOPPED

16 BABY SWEET CORN

100 G/4 OZ MANGE TOUT

2 CARROTS, THINLY SLICED

3 TBSP SOY SAUCE

1 TBSP TOASTED SESAME SEEDS

Bring a large saucepan of water to the boil, and add vermicelli with a dash of olive oil. Cook for about 5 minutes, stirring occasionally, until tender. Drain thoroughly and set aside.

Heat oil for deep frying, and pack one quarter of cooked vermicelli into a bird's nest, known as *nid d'oiseau*. (This is a small metal basket with long handles.) Otherwise, fry vermicelli in batches in a frying basket. Cook for 3 to 5 minutes in hot oil, until vermicelli is crisp and golden. Remove basket from bird's nest, and drain on kitchen paper. Repeat process to make three more baskets. Arrange baskets of loose vermicelli on individual serving plates. Set aside.

To make filling, heat sesame oil in a frying pan and sauté garlic. Add sweet corn, mange tout and carrots, stir, and cook for 3 to 5 minutes, until tender. Stir in soy sauce and sprinkle with sesame seeds. Cook for a further 2 minutes, then spoon into vermicelli baskets to serve.

tomato and
pasta timbales

Ingredients

SERVES 4

375 G/12 OZ DRIED,
MULTICOLOURED SPAGHETTINI

DASH OF OLIVE OIL,
PLUS EXTRA FOR GREASING

4 SMALL TOMATO SLICES

2 TBSP TOMATO PESTO

2 EGGS, BEATEN

100 ML/4 FL OZ MILK

SALT AND FRESHLY
GROUND BLACK PEPPER

SAUCE

225-G/8-OZ CARTON SIEVED
TOMATOES

1 TBSP SWEET SOY SAUCE

4 TBSP FRESH BASIL, CHOPPED

SALT AND FRESHLY
GROUND BLACK PEPPER

FRESH FLAT PARSLEY SPRIGS AND
CHERRY TOMATOES, TO GARNISH

Bring a large saucepan of water to the boil and add spaghettini with a dash of olive oil. Cook for about 10 minutes, stirring occasionally, until tender. Drain thoroughly and set aside to cool slightly.

Preheat oven to 160°C/325°F/Gas Mark 3. Grease four individual ovenproof moulds and place a circle of greaseproof paper in the bottom of each. Place a slice of tomato in base of each mould, then carefully pack in spaghettini, leaving a 5-mm/¼-in space at the top.

In a small bowl, combine tomato pesto, eggs, milk, salt and pepper. Beat well, then pour into each spaghettini mould, covering pasta. Arrange moulds in a roasting tin with enough boiling water to come halfway up sides. Bake for 40 minutes, or until set and firm to touch.

Meanwhile, to make the sauce, place all the ingredients in a saucepan and simmer, stirring, for 10 minutes, until thickened slightly.

Run a sharp knife around the edges of each timbale, then invert each on to individual plates. Pour a little sauce around the base of each timbale, and garnish with sprigs of parsley and cherry tomatoes.

stuffed peppers

Ingredients

SERVES 4

225 G/8 OZ GNOCCHETTI SARDI
(SMALL DUMPLING SHAPES)

DASH OF OLIVE OIL

4 PEPPERS, FOR STUFFING

FLAT LEAF PARSLEY SPRIGS,
TO GARNISH

FILLING

50 G/2 OZ BUTTER

6 SPRING ONIONS, FINELY CHOPPED

2 CLOVES OF GARLIC,
FINELY CHOPPED

1 PEPPER, SEEDED
AND FINELY DICED

SALT AND FRESHLY GROUND
BLACK PEPPER

75 G/3 OZ FRESHLY GRATED
PARMESAN CHEESE

Bring a large saucepan of water to the boil, and add gnocchetti sardi with a dash of olive oil. Cook for about 10 minutes, stirring occasionally, until tender. Drain thoroughly and set aside to cool slightly.

Preheat oven to 200°C/400°F/Gas Mark 6. Lay each pepper on its side and slice off top, reserving it to make lid. Scoop out and discard seeds and pith. Arrange peppers in a shallow, ovenproof dish, and set aside.

To make filling, melt butter in a frying pan and sauté spring onions and garlic for about 2 minutes, then add diced pepper. Season with salt and freshly ground black pepper and cook for 5 minutes, stirring occasionally.

Add gnocchetti and the Parmesan cheese to filling mixture, and cook for about 2 minutes to heat through. Using a spoon, stuff each pepper with pasta filling, scattering any extra around the edges.

Place pepper lids in dish and bake for about 30 minutes, until peppers have softened. Just before serving, place under grill for 2 to 3 minutes to char pepper skins, if desired. Serve garnished with parsley sprigs.

deep fried brie with salsa

Ingredients

SERVES 4

225 G/8 OZ FRENCH BRIE

1 EGG, BEATEN

100 G/4 OZ FRESH WHITE BREADCRUMBS

OIL FOR DEEP-FRYING

SALSA

1 TBSP SUNFLOWER OIL

1 SMALL ONION, FINELY CHOPPED

1 GRANNY'S BONNET OR OTHER MEDIUM-HOT RED CHILLI, SEEDED AND FINELY CHOPPED

1 RED JALAPEÑO CHILLI, SEEDED AND FINELY CHOPPED

100 G/4 OZ PRE-SOAKED APRICOTS, FINELY CHOPPED

150 ML/¼ PT ORANGE JUICE

FRESH SALAD LEAVES, TO GARNISH

Cut Brie into four equal portions. Dip in beaten egg, then coat in breadcrumbs. Cover and place in refrigerator while preparing the salsa.

Heat sunflower oil in a pan and gently sauté onion and chillies for 5 minutes. Add apricots and orange juice, and simmer for 15 minutes, or until the mixture reaches a chunky consistency.

Heat oil for deep-frying to 170°C/340°F and fry Brie for 3 to 4 minutes, or until golden. Drain on kitchen paper. Serve with apricot salsa, garnished with fresh salad leaves.

asparagus with red pepper sauce

Ingredients

SERVES 4

3 RED PEPPERS,
HALVED AND SEEDED

450 ML/³/₄ PT VEGETABLE
STOCK

1 TSP CHILLI SAUCE

JUICE OF 1 LEMON

1 GARLIC CLOVE,
FINELY CHOPPED

450 G/1 LB ASPARAGUS SPEARS,
TRIMMED

GRATED ZEST OF 1 LEMON

PARSLEY SPRIGS, TO GARNISH

To make sauce, cook peppers under a hot grill, skin side uppermost for 5 minutes until skin begins to blacken and blister. Transfer peppers to a covered bowl, seal and leave for about 10 minutes. Peel skin from peppers and discard.

Roughly chop peppers and put them in a saucepan with stock, chilli sauce, lemon juice and garlic. Cook over a gentle heat for 20 minutes or until peppers are tender. Transfer sauce to a food processor and blend for 10 to 15 seconds. Return purée to saucepan and heat through gently.

Meanwhile, tie asparagus spears into four equal bundles. Stand upright in a steamer or saucepan of boiling water and cook for 10 to 15 minutes until tender. Remove asparagus from pan and untie bundles. Arrange on four serving plates and spoon sauce over the top. Sprinkle with lemon zest, garnish with parsley and serve.

tomato and heart of palm slices

Ingredients

SERVES 4 TO 5

1 SQUARE WHITE SANDWICH LOAF

HEART OF PALM MAYONNAISE
AND CARROT MAYONNAISE

4 WHOLE EGGS

4 EGG YOLKS (SEE NOTE, P.4)

SALT

6 TBSP LIME JUICE

450-900 ML/15-30 FL OZ OLIVE
OIL

450 G/1 LB CANNED HEART OF
PALM, WITH 5 TBSP LIQUID

2 CARROTS, CHOPPED AND COOKED

1 TSP GROUND BLACK PEPPER

2 TSP PREPARED MUSTARD

TOMATO FILLING

3 LARGE ONIONS, FINELY SLICED

3 GARLIC CLOVES, FINELY CHOPPED

6 TOMATOES, BLENDED

5 TBSP FRESHLY GRATED
PARMESAN CHEESE

2 TBSP PLAIN FLOUR

SPINACH FILLING

450 G/1 LB SPINACH, FINELY
CHOPPED

225 ML/8 FL OZ MILK

SALT AND GROUND BLACK PEPPER

1 TBSP PLAIN FLOUR

Put loaf in freezer for 30 minutes, so it will be easier to slice. Using a bread knife, slice bread into 1-cm/½-in horizontal slices. Then make piles of two or three slices and remove crust.

For heart of palm mayonnaise and carrot mayonnaise, put eggs, yolks, salt and lime juice in a blender. In pulse mode, turn on and off for 5 seconds. Repeat. Turn on again and start pouring in olive oil, little by little. The mayonnaise will start to thicken.

When mayonnaise is ready, divide between two bowls. To one, add chopped heart of palm with reserved liquid. To the other, add chopped cooked carrots. Add half the pepper and mustard to each bowl.

For tomato filling, heat 3 tablespoons olive oil in a saucepan, and fry onions and garlic. When translucent, add blended tomatoes and Parmesan cheese. Cook for 10 minutes. Dissolve flour in a little water and pour onto tomatoes. This sauce should be thick, but remember it thickens when it cools. Adjust seasoning to taste.

For spinach filling, throw spinach into pan, pour in half of the milk, and cook for 5 minutes. Add salt and pepper. Dissolve flour in remaining milk and then add to pan. Stir continuously until a creamy consistency.

Now, place bottom slice of loaf on a rectangular plate and start to spread sauces over horizontal slices, alternating tomato, heart of palm, and spinach. Place top slice on top and, using a spatula, cover whole loaf with a generous layer of carrot mayonnaise.

Carefully insert some cocktail sticks through the layers and cover with cling film. Chill for 1 hour before serving. Serve with green salad leaves.

onion and green
pepper pie

Ingredients

SERVES 6

23-cm9-in PIE CRUST

175 G/6 oz PLAIN FLOUR

1/4 TSP SALT

50 G/2 oz SOLID VEGETABLE FAT

50 G/2 oz CHILLED BUTTER

ABOUT 3 TBSP ICED WATER

FILLING

2 LARGE YELLOW ONIONS

25 G/1 oz BUTTER

2 SMALL GREEN PEPPERS

225 G/8 oz GRATED MONTEREY JACK OR MILD CHEDDAR CHEESE

3 EGGS, LIGHTLY BEATEN

50 ML/4 FL oz SOURED CREAM

50 ML/4 FL oz MILK

1/4 TSP GROUND CUMIN

1/4 TSP WHITE PEPPER

1/2 TSP SALT

SLICED AVOCADO, TO GARNISH

To make crust, combine flour and salt. Using a pastry cutter or sharp knife, cut in shortening and butter until mixture has a coarse grain and tiny bits of shortening remaining. Sprinkle iced water over mixture, 1 tablespoon at a time, until dough forms a ball, that is not too sticky or overly stiff.

The dough will be easier to handle if you wrap the ball in cling film and refrigerate it for 20 to 30 minutes. Roll out dough on a lightly floured surface to about 30 cm/11 in diameter. Place dough in tart tin and unfold. Trim crust to a 2.5-cm/1-in overhang. Roll up overhang and pinch into a fluted edge. Refrigerate for 20 minutes, then bake in a 200°C/400°F/Gas Mark 6 oven until slightly browned, 12 to 14 minutes.

For filling, slice onions, then cut slices in half and separate rings. Melt butter in a frying pan. Add onions and sauté until golden brown, 20 to 25 minutes. While onions are cooking, prepare peppers. Roast peppers under a hot grill until the skin is blistered and charred. Place in a bowl, covered with a towel, for 10 minutes to cool, then peel, seed and chop.

Preheat oven to 180°C/350°F/Gas Mark 4. When onions are ready, mix in peppers, then put onion-pepper mixture in partially baked crust. Sprinkle cheese generously over onions.

Combine remaining ingredients except avocado. Pour the egg mixture over the onions and cheese. Bake pie until set and lightly brown, 40 to 45 minutes. Let it cool slightly, then serve warm, garnished with avocado.

selection of antipasti

braised artichokes

Ingredients

SERVES 4 TO 6

4 TBSP PARSLEY, FINELY CHOPPED

2-3 TBSP FRESH MINT
LEAVES, FINELY CHOPPED

8-10 GARLIC CLOVES,
FINELY CHOPPED

SALT AND PEPPER, TO TASTE

100 ML/4 FL OZ EXTRA-VIRGIN
OLIVE OIL

8 MEDIUM-SIZED ARTICHOKES

JUICE OF 1 LEMON

Combine parsley with mint, garlic, salt and pepper, and about
3 tablespoons of olive oil, or enough to form a paste. Leave to marinate
and develop the flavours while you prepare artichokes.

Remove hard leaves from artichokes, and cut away sharp top from
tender, inner leaves. Pull centre open, and scoop out thistly inside, using
a spoon and a sharp paring knife.

Stuff inside of each artichoke with herbed mixture, then lay artichokes in
a baking dish in a single layer. Sprinkle with salt, pepper and any leftover
mixture, then with remaining olive oil and lemon juice, adding enough
water to cover artichokes. Cover with a lid or with aluminium foil.

Bake in a preheated 180°C/350°F/Gas Mark 4 oven for about an hour.
Remove lid to taste sauce; if it lacks flavour, pour into a saucepan and
reduce until it condenses and intensifies. Season with salt, pepper and
lemon juice, then pour back over artichokes. Eat hot or cold.

roasted peppers in oil

Ingredients

SERVES 4

3 EACH: RED, YELLOW,
AND GREEN PEPPERS

1 TBSP SALT

100 ML/4 FL OZ WINE
VINEGAR

100 ML/4 FL OZ EXTRA-VIRGIN
OLIVE OIL

5 GARLIC CLOVES, CHOPPED

2 TSP PAPRIKA

1/2 TSP SUGAR, OR TO TASTE

Roast peppers by placing them on a
baking sheet under a preheated grill
for about 15 minutes on each side,
turning so that they char evenly.
Place in a covered bowl to steam for
about 10 minutes, then remove skins,
stems and seeds.

Cut peppers into halves lengthwise,
and combine them with their roasting
juices, salt, vinegar, olive oil, garlic,
paprika and sugar, as desired. Leave
to chill for at least 2 hours, or
overnight if possible, before serving.

italian-style marinated carrots

Ingredients

SERVES 4

8-10 MEDIUM-SIZED CARROTS

3-5 GARLIC CLOVES, CHOPPED

3 TBSP EXTRA-VIRGIN
OLIVE OIL

2 TBSP RASPBERRY VINEGAR

3-5 TBSP PARSELY, CHOPPED

SALT AND PEPPER TO TASTE

Cut carrots into about 5-mm/¼-in thick slices. Steam or boil them until they are tender, about 15 minutes, Drain well, then toss with remaining ingredients and serve.

stuffed mushrooms

Ingredients

MAKES 14 TO 16 MUSHROOMS

375 G/12 OZ LARGE MUSHROOMS

25 G/1 OZ CRUMBLED FETA CHEESE

4 TBSP BREADCRUMBS

1/2 TSP OLIVE OIL (PLUS OIL FOR BRUSHING THE MUSHROOMS)

1 TSP LIGHT SOY SAUCE

1/2 TSP GROUND THYME

1 TSP GRATED ONION

3 TSP CAPERS, DRAINED

Wash mushrooms and remove stems. Add 3 tablespoons of cheese, together with breadcrumbs, and mix thoroughly. Stir in olive oil and soy sauce. When well blended, stir in thyme, grated onion and capers.

Preheat grill. Brush mushroom caps with olive oil, inside and out. Stuff with breadcrumb mixture. Then crumble remaining feta over mushrooms. Grill until heated thoroughly, and tops have begun to brown, about 6 to 8 minutes.

spanish salad of frisée

Ingredients

SERVES 4

1 SMALL HEAD OF FRISÉE, CLEANED AND CORED, CUT INTO BITE-SIZED PIECES

2 ROASTED, RED PEPPERS, PEELED AND CUT INTO STRIPS (SEE P.50)

75 G/3 OZ RIPE SPANISH CABRALES, A BLUE CHEESE, CRUMBLED (OR OTHER BLUE CHEESE TYPE IF UNAVAILABLE)

10–15 PIMIENTO-STUFFED GREEN OLIVES

3 TBSP EXTRA-VIRGIN OLIVE OIL

1 TBSP SHERRY VINEGAR

Arrange frisée, and garnish with roasted peppers, blue cheese and green olives. Dress with olive oil and sherry vinegar.

pear gorgonzola salad

Ingredients

SERVES 4

1 HEAD COS LETTUCE,
WASHED, SEPARATED,
AND TRIMMED

2 PEARS

2 AVOCADOS

50 G/**2** OZ CRUMBLED
GORGONZOLA CHEESE

65 G/**2**½ OZ FLAKED
ALMONDS

VINAIGRETTE OF YOUR CHOICE

Divide lettuce leaves among six plates. Cut unpeeled pears into thin lengthwise wedges, and core. Peel avocados and cut into thin lengthwise wedges. Alternate pear and avocado slices in sunburst arrangement on each plate. Sprinkle cheese and almonds over salad. Serve drizzled with vinaigrette.

spring rolls

Ingredients

SERVES 4

3 TBSP PEANUT OIL,
PLUS EXTRA FOR BRUSHING

1 AUBERGINE, SLICED

1 SMALL ONION, FINELY SLICED

3 TBSP OYSTER SAUCE

100 ML/4 FL OZ WATER

225 G/8 OZ PREPARED
STIR-FRY VEGETABLES

SALT

8 SHEETS FILO PASTRY, MEASURING
ABOUT 22 x 30 CM/7 x 12 IN

SOY SAUCE

Heat oil in a pan, add aubergine and onion and cook gently until oil has
been absorbed. Mix oyster sauce with water, add to pan and continue to
cook slowly for about 10 minutes, until aubergine is tender. Remove from
heat and leave until cool enough to handle.

Preheat oven to 200°C/400°F/Gas Mark 6 and lightly oil a baking sheet.
Mix aubergine and onion with stir-fry vegetables, adding a little salt if
necessary. Fold filo sheets in half and brush with oil to keep them moist.
Divide vegetable mixture between them and sprinkle each with soy sauce.

Fold bottom and sides of the pastry in over filling, then roll pastry up into
a sausage, brushing edges with a little oil. Place on prepared baking
sheet and brush lightly with oil again. Bake spring rolls in preheated oven
for 10 to 15 minutes, until pastry is browned and crisp. Serve immediately
with a rich soy sauce good for dipping.

chinese vegetable and
omelette salad

Ingredients

SERVES 4

450 G/1 LB YOUNG CABBAGE

OIL FOR DEEP FRYING

1 TSP SALT

1/2 TSP GROUND CINNAMON

100 G/4 OZ BEAN SPROUTS

4 SPRING ONIONS, HALVED
LENGTHWISE

6 CANNED WATER CHESTNUTS,
DRAINED AND CHOPPED

1 RED PEPPER, SLICED

1 YELLOW PEPPER, SLICED

40 G/1 1/2 OZ SALTED CASHEW NUTS

OMELETTE

2 EGGS

1/2 TSP CHINESE 5-SPICE POWDER

DRESSING

2 TBSP LIGHT SOY SAUCE

1 TBSP LIME JUICE

1 TBSP SESAME OIL

1/2 TSP GROUND GINGER

Finely shred young cabbage. Heat oil in a wok and deep-fry cabbage for 4 to 5 minutes. Drain well on kitchen paper, and sprinkle with salt and cinnamon. Place in a large serving bowl. Top with bean sprouts, spring onions, water chestnuts, peppers and cashew nuts.

Beat eggs for omelette with Chinese 5-spice powder. Heat and oil a 18-cm/6-in omelette pan, then pour in eggs, tilting pan to coat base with egg. Cook for 2 minutes until top is set. Flip over and cook for 2 minutes more. Remove and cut into strips. Sprinkle over vegetables. Whisk dressing ingredients together, drizzle over salad, and serve.

sample it

fish & seafood

fish bites

Ingredients

SERVES 4

300 G/10 OZ WHITE FISH, CUBED

2 TBSP LIGHT SOY SAUCE

1 TBSP LEMON JUICE

2 TBSP DRY WHITE WINE

1/2 TSP GROUND GINGER

1 LARGE COURGETTE

1 LARGE CARROT

1 TBSP FRESH DILL,
CHOPPED TO GARNISH

SAUCE

150 ML/1/4 PT DRY WHITE WINE

5 TBSP FISH STOCK

1 TBSP LIGHT SOY SAUCE

2 TBSP GINGER WINE

1 TSP ROOT GINGER,
FINELY CHOPPED

1 TBSP CORNFLOUR

2 SPRING ONIONS, CHOPPED

Place fish in a shallow dish. Mix soy sauce, lemon juice, white wine and ginger. Pour over fish, cover and marinate for 2 hours.

Meanwhile, using a vegetable peeler, slice courgette and carrot lengthwise into thin strips. Blanch vegetables in boiling water for 1 minute, and then plunge them into cold water. Leave until cold. Soak four wooden skewers in cold water for 30 minutes so they do not char in cooking.

Remove fish from marinade, reserving liquid together with vegetable strips. Pat vegetables dry with kitchen paper. Wrap a piece of courgette around each fish cube, and then a piece of carrot. Thread four cubes onto each wooden skewer, and brush them with marinade. Grill for 10 minutes, turning once, and rebrushing with marinade.

To make sauce, bring wine, stock, soy sauce, ginger wine and ginger to the boil in a pan. Blend cornflour with 2 tablespoons of cold water, and then add to pan. Return to the boil until thickened, add spring onions and cook for 1 minute. Sprinkle with dill, and then serve with fish bites.

giant prawn gratin in pineapple shell

Ingredients

SERVES 4

1 LARGE PINEAPPLE

1 KG/2¼ LB DUBLIN BAY PRAWNS

SALT AND GROUND WHITE PEPPER

MIXED HERBS, TO TASTE

100 ML/4 FL OZ DRY WHITE WINE

40 G/1½ OZ BUTTER

4 SHALLOTS, FINELY CHOPPED

4 GARLIC CLOVES, FINELY CHOPPED

100 G/4 OZ MUSHROOMS

100 ML/4 FL OZ DOUBLE CREAM

3 TBSP FRESH PARSLEY, CHOPPED

1 CHRISTOPHENE, CUBED AND
BOILED, OR 450 G/1 LB FRESH
PEAS, COOKED

2 SMALL CARROTS, COOKED AND
CUT INTO FINE STRIPS

A LITTLE GRATED PARMESAN CHEESE

Cut pineapple in half lengthwise, including through crown. Using a sharp knife, make a few cuts lengthwise to make it easy to remove flesh. Chop flesh and reserve. Place pineapple halves upside-down to drain.

Wash prawns. Tie some string around them lengthwise, to fold tails inside. Put plenty of water in a large saucepan with some salt, mixed herbs and wine. Bring to the boil and throw prawns in pan. Cook for 8 to 10 minutes, or until slightly reddish-pink.

Drain and let cool. Cut off string and, with kitchen scissors, make a cut into central part of belly. Scoop out meat, cutting it into chunks. Remove dark strip located along belly and discard.

Preheat a 190°C/375°F/Gas Mark 5 oven. Melt butter in a frying pan and fry shallots. Add garlic, mushrooms and salt and pepper. Reduce heat, add prawns and cream. Let cook for 5 minutes and season. Add parsley, christophene or peas and carrots. Remove from heat and add pineapple.

Pat pineapple skins dry and then fill with the mixture. Scatter a little Parmesan on top and bake in oven for 15 minutes until golden.

noodles with japanese fishcake

Ingredients

SERVES 4

2 SLICES JAPANESE FISH CAKE

1 CARROT

1 LEEK

100 G/4 OZ MANGE TOUT

$^1/_4$ HEAD CHINESE LEAVES

375 G/12 OZ UDON NOODLES

SALT

150 ML/$^1/_4$ PT CHICKEN STOCK

12 LARGE, COOKED PRAWNS

DIPPING SAUCE

6 TBSP JAPANESE SOY SAUCE

2 TBSP SAKE

1 TSP SUGAR

150 ML/$^1/_4$ PT JAPANESE-STYLE STOCK

SMALL PINCH OF WASABI (HOT HORSERADISH SAUCE)

1 SPRING ONION, FINELY CHOPPED

First prepare dipping sauce. Heat soy sauce, sake, sugar and stock, stirring until sugar dissolves. Bring to the boil, then remove from heat, and let cool. Add wasabi, stir in spring onion, then pour sauce into small dishes.

Now, prepare noodles, fish cake and vegetables. Cut fish cake, carrot and leek into matchstick-sized strips. Top and tail mange tout, and finely shred Chinese leaves. Cook noodles in boiling salted water until tender. Meanwhile, bring chicken stock to the boil. Add carrot and leek, and simmer for 1 minute. Then add mange tout, and cook for a further minute. Finally, add Chinese leaves, and bring back to the boil. Add prawns, and remove pan from the heat. Leave to stand for 2 minutes.

Drain noodles, and divide them between four bowls. Carefully spoon vegetables and prawns over noodles; then pour over stock. Top with pieces of fish cake, and serve immediately.

smoked salmon timbales

Ingredients

SERVES 4

TIMBALES

175 G/6 OZ SOUP PASTA

100 G/4 OZ RICOTTA CHEESE

100 G/4 OZ SMOKED SALMON, CHOPPED

2 TBSP CHIVES, CHOPPED

1 TBSP PARSLEY, FINELY CHOPPED

1 LARGE EGG, BEATEN

GRATED ZEST OF HALF A LEMON

SALT AND FRESHLY GROUND BLACK PEPPER

SPINACH SAUCE

25 G/1 OZ BUTTER

1 SMALL ONION, FINELY CHOPPED

2 TBSP FLOUR

150 ML/¼ PT MILK

225 G/8 OZ FRESH SPINACH LEAVES, WASHED

FRESHLY GRATED NUTMEG

Preheat oven to 180°C/350°F/Gas Mark 4. Base-line four individual soufflé dishes with greaseproof paper, and place on a baking sheet.

Cook the soup pasta in boiling salted water until tender. Drain well. Mix pasta, ricotta, smoked salmon, chives, parsley, egg, lemon zest, and salt and pepper to taste. Spoon mixture into prepared dishes, pressing it down well. Cover with circles of greaseproof paper, and bake in preheated oven for 30 minutes, or until mixture has set.

Meanwhile, make spinach sauce. Melt butter in a saucepan. Add onion, and cook for 10 minutes, stirring, until softened. Stir in flour, then add milk, and bring to the boil, stirring. Add spinach, stir well, and cover pan. Simmer gently for 5 minutes, stirring occasionally. Purée sauce in a blender, then add salt, pepper and nutmeg to taste. Rinse out pan, return sauce to pan, and reheat if necessary.

Pour some sauce onto warmed serving plates. Remove paper from tops and slide a knife around the edge of timbales. Invert onto spinach sauce; then remove remaining paper before serving.

stuffed mussels

Ingredients

SERVES 4

20 LARGE GREEN-LIPPED MUSSELS, ON THE HALF SHELL

4 TBSP OLIVE OIL

1 LARGE ONION, FINELY CHOPPED

1 RED CHILLI, SEEDED AND FINELY CHOPPED

1 SMALL AUBERGINE, FINELY CHOPPED

2 GARLIC CLOVES, FINELY CHOPPED

SALT AND FRESHLY GROUND BLACK PEPPER

50 G/2 OZ FRESH WHOLEWHEAT BREADCRUMBS

FRESH PARSLEY, CHOPPED, TO GARNISH

Preheat oven to 220°C/425°F/Gas Mark 7. Loosen mussels on the half shells and arrange them on a large baking sheet.

Heat oil in a large pan. Add onion and chilli and cook until starting to soften, then add aubergine and garlic. Continue cooking for 5 to 6 minutes, until all vegetables are soft and lightly browned. Season well, then add fresh breadcrumbs and mix thoroughly.

Pile a teaspoonful of filling into each shell over the mussel, then bake In hot oven for 12 to 15 minutes, until piping hot. Serve immediately, with chopped parsley to garnish.

tuna and aubergine kebabs

Ingredients

SERVES 4

600 G/20 OZ FRESH TUNA STEAK, CUT INTO 2.5-CM/1-IN CUBES

1 LONG, THIN, JAPANESE-STYLE AUBERGINE

MARINADE

GRATED ZEST AND JUICE OF 1 LIME

1 TBSP OLIVE OIL

1 GARLIC CLOVE, FINELY CHOPPED

2 TBSP FRESH OREGANO AND PARSLEY, CHOPPED

SALT AND FRESHLY GROUND BLACK PEPPER

Place tuna in a non-metallic bowl, then add all marinade ingredients. Stir well and leave for at least 1 hour, stirring once or twice.

Half cook aubergine on barbecue or under grill, until skin is just starting to wrinkle. Cut into thick slices.

Soak kebab sticks in water to prevent them charring under grill. Thread tuna and aubergine on skewers, then brush with remaining marinade.

Cook under a moderate heat for 5 to 6 minutes on each side, either on barbecue or under grill, basting at intervals with any remaining marinade. Serve alone or with a rice salad.

crab and red pepper tartlets

Ingredients

SERVES 3 TO 4

50 G/2 OZ BUTTER

3 RED PEPPERS, SEEDED AND
CUT LENGTHWISE INTO THIN
STRIPS

1 TBSP DILL, CHOPPED

4 SHEETS FILO PASTRY,
DEFROSTED IF FROZEN

50 G/2 OZ PARMESAN
CHEESE, FRESHLY GRATED

225 G/8 OZ FRESH WHITE
CRABMEAT

2 TBSP MAYONNAISE

1 TBSP LEMON OR LIME JUICE

In a large frying pan over a medium heat, melt 2 tablespoons of butter. Add red pepper strips and cook until softened. Remove from heat and stir in dill until thoroughly mixed.

Preheat oven to 180°C/350°F/Gas Mark 4. Lightly grease eight 6 x 3-cm/2½ x 1¼-in muffin tin cups. Stack filo pastry on a work surface and cut into 10-cm/4-in squares.

Place one square on a work surface and brush lightly with a little butter; do not brush right up to the edge. Sprinkle with a little Parmesan. Place a second square on top of first at a right angle, to create a star shape. Brush lightly with butter and sprinkle with a little Parmesan. Top with a third square, at an angle to first two, but do not brush with butter. Ease into one of the muffin tin cups, keeping edges pointing up to form a flat-bottomed tulip shape. (Keep the filo pastry sheets you aren't working with covered with a damp teatowel to prevent them from drying out.) Line remaining cups.

Bake until crisp and golden, about 10 minutes. Transfer to a wire rack to cool slightly. Carefully remove each filo case and set on a wire rack to cool. Divide pepper mixture evenly among tartlet cases and top each with a little crabmeat. Mix mayonnaise with lemon or lime juice and drizzle a little sauce over crabmeat. Garnish with miniature dill sprigs.

hawaiian coconut prawns

Ingredients

SERVES 6

675 G/1¹/₂ LB JUMBO PRAWNS

2 TBSP HOISIN SAUCE

4 TBSP FRESH LIME JUICE

1 TBSP ROOT GINGER, GRATED

175 G/6 OZ PLAIN FLOUR

¹/₂ TSP SALT

2 EGGS

1 TBSP VEGETABLE OIL

225 G/8 FL OZ FLAT BEER

APPROX 50 G/2 OZ PLAIN FLOUR
FOR DIPPING

175 G/6 OZ COCONUT, SHREDDED

OIL FOR DEEP-FRYING

Shell and devein prawns, leaving tails intact. Cut lengthwise through underside of prawns so that top half opens up like butterfly wings. In a small bowl, combine Hoisin sauce, lime juice and ginger. Put prawns in a non-metallic bowl and toss with marinade. Cover and refrigerate at least 2 hours, stirring once or twice, to allow flavours to develop.

The batter also benefits from being made in advance. Combine flour and salt. In another bowl, lightly beat eggs with a fork, then add oil and beer. Stir liquid into flour until you have a slightly lumpy batter. Refrigerate batter until you are ready to cook prawns.

Drain prawns. Stir marinade into batter. Lay out ingredients in this order: prawns, dipping flour in a small bowl, batter, coconut in a bowl and a large, clean plate. Dip prawns into flour and shake off any excess. Dip prawns into batter and let excess drip off. Roll prawns in coconut and pat on additional coconut if necessary. Put prawns on plate.

Pour 7.5 cm/3 in of oil into a heavy pan and heat to about 185°C/365°F. Fry prawns in batches until golden brown, about 1 minute. Drain and serve with a dipping sauce of your choice, such as that on page 77.

mussels vinaigrette

Ingredients

SERVES 4

20-24 SMALL MUSSELS

225 ML/8 FL OZ DRY WHITE WINE

225 ML/8 FL OZ WATER

100 ML/4 FL OZ RED WINE VINEGAR

1 GARLIC CLOVE, FINELY CHOPPED

2 TSP DIJON MUSTARD

150 ML/¹⁄₄ PT OLIVE OIL

¹⁄₄ TSP SALT

¹⁄₈ TSP PEPPER

2 TBSP FRESH PARSLEY, CHOPPED

225 G/8 OZ YOUNG SPINACH LEAVES

4 SLICES OF SWEET ONION, SEPARATED INTO RINGS

50 G/2 OZ TOASTED HAZELNUTS, COARSELY CHOPPED

Scrub mussels with a brush to remove grit. Remove beards. Discard any mussels that do not close and put remaining mussels in a pot. Add wine and water. Bring to the boil, cover and reduce heat. Simmer for 5 to 7 minutes until mussels open. Discard any that did not open. Put cooked mussels in a shallow, non-metallic dish.

While mussels are cooking, make vinaigrette. Combine red wine vinegar, garlic, mustard, olive oil, salt, pepper and parsley. Whisk until well-blended. Pour over hot mussels. Cover and refrigerate for at least 6 hours, occasionally spooning marinade over mussels.

About 30 minutes before serving, remove mussels from refrigerator to return to room temperature. Divide spinach amongst four plates. Top with onion rings and hazelnuts. Divide mussels among the plates, spoon vinaigrette marinade over salads and serve.

pan-cooked
prawn kebabs

Ingredients

SERVES 4

8–12 MEDIUM TOMATOES

PINCH OF SUGAR

PINCH OF SALT

35–40 JUMBO PRAWNS, IN THEIR SHELLS, HEADS AND TAILS REMOVED (OPTIONAL)

6–8 TBSP EXTRA-VIRGIN OLIVE OIL

2 TBSP BALSAMIC VINEGAR

3 GARLIC CLOVES, CHOPPED

SALT AND BLACK PEPPER, TO TASTE

2–3 TBSP FRESH BASIL LEAVES, TORN

LEMON WEDGES, TO SERVE

Preheat oven to 190°C/375°F/Gas Mark 5. Place tomatoes in a roasting dish, preferably a ceramic Mediterranean one, then bake uncovered, for 20 to 30 minutes. The skin should have split, exposing some flesh. Sprinkle with sugar and salt, then return to oven and continue to roast for another 15 to 25 minutes.

Remove and let cool. It is best to let them sit overnight, as the juices will run out and thicken. Remove skins of tomatoes, and squeeze them to extract their flavourful juices. Discard squeezed-out skins, and pour juices over roasted tomatoes, then cut into halves or quarters.

Place prawns in a non-metallic bowl for marinating; add several tablespoons of olive oil, a teaspoon of balsamic vinegar, and half the garlic. Leave for at least 30 minutes. Soak eight to twelve bamboo skewers in cold water (or use metal skewers to avoid soaking).Tightly thread prawns onto skewers. Save marinade to heat through as a pan sauce.

Heat a skillet and brown prawns quickly on each side, for only a few minutes, depending on their size. Remove to a plate, and keep warm in a low oven.

Heat tomatoes in pan, then remove to plate, and sprinkle with remaining garlic. Pour marinade into pan, heat through until it bubbles, then pour over prawn skewers and tomatoes. Sprinkle with salt and pepper, then basil and serve right away, accompanied by lemon wedges.

middle eastern
swordfish kebabs

Ingredients

SERVES 4

1.25 KG/2¹/₂ LB SWORDFISH

1 ONION, GRATED

8 GARLIC CLOVES, CHOPPED

JUICE OF 2 LEMONS

100 ML/4 FL OZ OLIVE OIL

SEVERAL BAY LEAVES

SALT AND PEPPER

TAHINI SAUCE

175 G/6 OZ TAHINI (SESAME PASTE)

2 GARLIC CLOVES, CHOPPED

FEW DASHES OF HOT-PEPPER SAUCE

FEW PINCHES OF CUMIN

SALT AND PEPPER

JUICE OF 1 LEMON

2 TBSP EXTRA-VIRGIN OLIVE OIL

100 ML/4 FL OZ WATER, OR ENOUGH
TO MAKE A SMOOTH, THICK SAUCE

FEW SPRIGS OF FRESH OREGANO

LEMON WEDGES, TO GARNISH

Combine fish, onion, garlic, lemon juice, olive oil, bay leaves, salt and pepper. Marinate for at least an hour, preferably overnight in refrigerator.

Skewer marinated fish and bay leaves on either soaked bamboo (30 minutes in cold water) or metal skewers, alternating fish cubes with bay leaves. Though you don't eat bay leaves, they perfume the fish delightfully. Grill over a medium-low charcoal fire for about 8 minutes, turning to cook evenly, or cook under a preheated grill.

Meanwhile, mix tahini with garlic, hot-pepper sauce, cumin, salt, pepper, lemon juice and olive oil, then slowly stir in water until it reaches desired consistency. Taste for seasoning and adjust, if necessary.

Serve swordfish kebabs with sprigs of fresh oregano, accompanied by lemon wedges and a serving of tahini sauce on the side.

anticipate i

meat & poultry

thai lettuce parcels

Ingredients

SERVES 4

DIPPING SAUCE

2 TBSP THAI FISH SAUCE

2 GARLIC CLOVES, FINELY CHOPPED

1–2 TBSP SUGAR

2 TBSP LIME JUICE

2 TBSP WHITE WINE VINEGAR

1 BIRD'S EYE (THAI) CHILLI,
SEEDED AND FINELY CHOPPED

PARCELS

1 TBSP CORN OR SUNFLOWER OIL

1 GARLIC CLOVE, FINELY CHOPPED

2 LEMON GRASS STALKS,
OUTER LEAVES REMOVED AND
FINELY CHOPPED

1-INCH PIECE ROOT GINGER,
PEELED AND FINELY CHOPPED

2–3 BIRD'S EYE (THAI) RED
CHILLIES, SEEDED AND CHOPPED

225 G/8 OZ CHICKEN BREAST,
SKINNED AND FINELY SLICED

1 TBSP SOY SAUCE

2 TSP THAI FISH SAUCE

100 G/4 OZ BEAN SPROUTS

1 SMALL ICEBERG LETTUCE, RINSED

Thoroughly mix all ingredients for dipping sauce together and leave for at least 30 minutes for flavours to develop and intensify.

Heat oil in a wok or large saucepan and stir-fry garlic, lemon grass, ginger, and chillies for 2 minutes. Add chicken and continue to stir-fry for 5 minutes, or until chicken is cooked. Add soy and fish sauce, stir once, then add bean sprouts and stir-fry for a further 30 seconds.

Arrange spoonfuls of chicken mixture on a lettuce leaf and drizzle with a little of the sauce. Roll up to form a parcel and serve.

aubergine and
chicken strips

Ingredients

SERVES 4

SPICED FLOUR

50 G/2 OZ WHOLEWHEAT FLOUR

2 TSP GROUND CINNAMON

2 TSP PAPRIKA

1 TSP SALT

STICKS

1 EGG WHITE

1 TBSP DOUBLE CREAM

VEGETABLE OIL FOR DEEP-FRYING

1 LARGE AUBERGINE,
CUT INTO THIN STRIPS

2 LARGE CHICKEN BREASTS,
CUT INTO THIN STRIPS

3 TBSP SESAME SEEDS

SALT

LEMON WEDGES, TARTARE SAUCE OR
MAYONNAISE TO SERVE

Mix flour with spices and salt in a shallow dish. Beat egg white with a fork until just frothy, then mix it with double cream.

Heat oil for frying to 190°C/375°F in a large pan. Dip aubergine and chicken strips in cream mixture, then turn them in spiced flour to coat well.

Deep-fry aubergine and chicken in batches until golden, then drain on kitchen paper. Scatter with sesame seeds and salt and serve with lemon wedges, and a serving of tartare sauce or mayonnaise.

potted ham with aubergines

Ingredients

SERVES 4

2 LARGE AUBERGINES

SALT AND FRESHLY
GROUND BLACK PEPPER

150 ML/¼ PT MILK

12 G/½ OZ BUTTER

1 TBSP PLAIN FLOUR

2 TSP DIJON OR
PEPPER MUSTARD

OLIVE OIL FOR FRYING
AND GREASING

4 TBSP DRY WHITE WINE

1 TSP POWDERED GELATIN

150 G/5 OZ COOKED HAM,
CHOPPED

150 ML/¼ PT DOUBLE CREAM

2 TBSP FRESH PARSLEY,
CHOPPED

Slice one aubergine very thinly. Lay slices on a baking sheet in a single layer, sprinkle with salt, then leave for 30 minutes. Cook the other aubergine over a barbecue, under a grill, or in a hot oven until skin is wrinkled and flesh is tender; turn once or twice during cooking. Cover with a damp cloth and leave for about 10 minutes, then peel off skin.

Heat milk, butter and flour together in a pan until thickened and boiling, stirring all the time. Add mustard, salt and pepper, then remove from heat, cover with greaseproof paper to prevent a skin forming, and leave until cold.

Rinse salted aubergine thoroughly and pat dry on kitchen paper. Heat a little oil, then cook aubergine slices on both sides, a few at a time, until tender, adding more oil as necessary. Drain on kitchen paper and leave to cool.

Heat wine in a small pan until bubbling, then remove from heat and sprinkle on gelatin. Stir to dissolve, then leave for 2 to 3 minutes. Oil four individual bowls and line them with aubergine slices, overlapping them slightly around the sides.

Cut peeled aubergine into chunks, then purée it with ham in a blender or food processor. Whip cream until thick and floppy. Mix cream and ham mixture into sauce, blending well. Season with pepper; the ham should provide all the salt required. Stir gelatin again, then fold it into the ham cream with a generous half of the parsley.

Carefully spoon ham into prepared moulds, banging them on worktop to shake mixture down. Chill for at least 2 hours before turning out the moulds onto individual plates. Sprinkle with remaining parsley and serve with toast and salad.

sweet and sour pork won tons

Ingredients

SERVES 4

ABOUT **175 G/6 OZ LEAN, BONELESS PORK**

PINCH OF **CHINESE 5-SPICE POWDER**

1 TSP SESAME OIL

1 GARLIC CLOVE, FINELY CHOPPED

1 TBSP SOY SAUCE

18 SQUARES WON TON DOUGH OR READY-MADE WRAPPERS

1 EGG, BEATEN

OIL, FOR DEEP-FRYING

SWEET AND SOUR SAUCE, TO SERVE

Cut pork into 1-cm/$\frac{1}{2}$-in cubes. Place the cubes of meat in a non-metallic bowl, and sprinkle with a good pinch of 5-spice powder, sesame oil, garlic and soy sauce. Let marinate for a few hours, allowing time for meat to become well-flavoured with spices.

Brush the middle of a square of won ton dough or a wrapper with a little egg, and place a piece of meat on it. Then gather dough around meat to make a tiny bundle with fluted edges. Fill and shape all the won tons in the same way. Then make Sweet and Sour sauce as given on page 77.

Heat sufficient oil to deep-fry won tons to 190°C/375°F, or until a cube of day-old bread browns in about 30 seconds. Fry won tons, a few at a time, until they have puffed up, are golden and cooked through. Drain well on kitchen paper. Serve immediately with Sweet and Sour sauce.

sweet and sour
dipping sauce

Ingredients

SERVES 4

2 TBSP OIL

1 TSP SESAME OIL

1 LARGE ONION, ROUGHLY CHOPPED

1 LARGE GREEN PEPPER, SEEDED AND DICED

1 LARGE CARROT, CUT INTO MATCHSTICK STRIPS

6 TBSP TOMATO KETCHUP

150 ML/¼ PT DRY SHERRY

2 TBSP SUGAR

4 TBSP CIDER VINEGAR

4 TBSP SOY SAUCE

225-G/8-OZ CAN PINEAPPLE RINGS IN SYRUP

2 TSP CORNFLOUR

Heat both oils in a saucepan. Add onion, green pepper and carrot. Stir-fry vegetables for 5 minutes, until they are lightly cooked, but still firm.

Stir in tomato ketchup, sherry, sugar, vinegar and soy sauce. Drain pineapple, and mix a little syrup with cornflour to make a smooth, thin paste. Add remaining syrup; then pour this mixture into sauce.

Bring to the boil, stirring all the time, then reduce heat, and simmer for 5 minutes. Cut pineapple rings into chunks, and add them to sauce. Remove from heat, and serve.

rich egg pasta dough

Ingredients

MAKES 675 G/1½ LB PASTA

450 G/1 LB STRONG WHITE FLOUR

1 TSP SALT

4-5 LARGE EGGS

Mix flour and salt in a bowl, making a well in the middle. Beat eggs, then pour two thirds into the well in flour.

Gradually mix in the flour, adding more egg until mixture clumps together. The dough may need 4 to 5 eggs to get the right consistency for a firm, manageable dough, depending on slight variations in absorbency of flour.

Mix and knead dough until smooth and pliable, and let sit before using.

kreplach

Ingredients

MAKES 72

350 G/12 OZ EGG PASTA DOUGH

2 TBSP BEEF DRIPPING

1 SMALL ONION, GRATED

SALT AND FRESHLY
GROUND BLACK PEPPER

175 G/6 OZ GROUND,
LEAN ROAST BEEF

1 TBSP PARSLEY, FINELY CHOPPED

1 TBSP BEEF GRAVY

1 EGG, BEATEN

First, make rich egg pasta dough as given on page 77, and set it aside to rest while you make filling.

Melt dripping in a saucepan. Add onion, and cook, stirring, for 5 to 8 minutes, or until some of moisture has evaporated, and onion has lost its raw taste. Remove from heat, and stir in salt and pepper to taste. Then add beef, parsley and gravy, which will bind mixture. Taste for seasoning.

Cut dough in half. Roll out one half to form a square slightly larger than 30 cm/12 in. Trim edges; then cut dough into 5-cm/2-in wide strips and across into 5-cm/2-in squares. Brush squares with beaten egg. Place a little filling in the middle of each square until you have used half of the mixture; then fold one corner of dough over to enclose filling, forming a triangular-shaped piece of pasta. Pinch edges of dough together well. Repeat with the remaining dough and filling.

Cook Kreplach in boiling salted water, for about 3 minutes, until tender. Drain and serve with soup. Kreplach may also be served with a rich tomato sauce or gravy.

empanadas

Ingredients

SERVES **6**

75 G/3 OZ GROUND PORK

75 G/3 OZ GROUND BEEF

1 SMALL ONION, FINELY CHOPPED

2 MILD JALAPEÑO CHILLIES, SEEDED
AND FINELY CHOPPED

¹/₂ SMALL RED PEPPER,
SEEDED AND FINELY CHOPPED

¹/₂ SMALL GREEN PEPPER, SEEDED
AND FINELY CHOPPED

¹/₂ TSP GROUND CLOVES

1 TSP GROUND CINNAMON

1 TBSP TOMATO PURÉE

5 TBSP WATER

1 TSP CLEAR HONEY

JUICE OF **1** LIME

675 G/1¹/₂ LB FROZEN SHORTCRUST
PASTRY, DEFROSTED

OIL FOR DEEP-FRYING

Put pork and beef into a nonstick frying pan and cook over a gentle heat, stirring constantly, for 8 minutes, or until meat has browned.

Add onion and chillies, and cook for 5 minutes, stirring frequently. Add both peppers and spices, and cook for a further 3 minutes. Blend tomato purée with water and add to pan, together with honey and lime juice. Bring to the boil, then simmer for 15 minutes, stirring frequently, or until most of liquid has evaporated. Allow to cool.

Roll pastry out on a lightly floured surface and cut out twelve 10-cm/4-in circles. Divide filling between pastry circles, brush edges with water and fold over to make small pastries. Pinch edges together.

Heat oil to 180°C/350°F and fry Empanadas, a few at a time, for 3 minutes or until golden brown. Drain on kitchen paper and serve with a red or green chilli sauce, green salad leaves and lime wedges.

index

Andalusian salsa 30
antipasti 50
artichokes, braised 50
asparagus with red pepper
   sauce 45
aubergine
   aubergine and chicken
      strips 73
   aubergine guacamole 24
   aubergine toasts 37
   potted ham with
      aubergine 75
   tuna and aubergine
      kebabs 63
avocado salsa 26
beef
   empanadas 79
   kreplach 78
beer mustard bread 10
black olive tapenade 32
braised artichokes 50
bread
   bagels 14
   beer mustard bread 10
   crisp breadsticks 11
   rye crescent rolls 15
carrots, Italian-style
marinated 51
cheese
   deep fried Brie with
      salsa 44
   nut and cheese pepper
      slices 20
   pear Gorgonzola salad 54
   Spanish salad of frisée 53
chicken
   aubergine and chicken
      strips 73
   Thai lettuce parcels 72
   Thai spiced chicken
      soup 17
Chinese vegetable and
   omelette salad 56
couscous soup, Lebanese 16
crab and sweetcorn soup 18
crab and red pepper
   tartlets 64
Cretan sandwich 36
crisp breadsticks 11
crostini 40
deep fried Brie with salsa 44
empanadas 79
fish bites 58
Giant Prawn gratin in
   pineapple shell 59
guacamole, aubergine 24
   traditional 23
ham with aubergine,
   potted 75
Hawaiian coconut prawns 66
heart of palm slices, tomato
   and 46
homemade tortilla chips 31
hummus 22
Italian-style marinated
   carrots 51
Japanese fishcake, noodles
   with 60

kebabs, Middle Eastern
   swordfish 70
   pan-cooked prawn 68
   tuna and aubergine 63
kreplach 78
Lebanese couscous soup 16
lettuce parcels, Thai 72
Middle Eastern swordfish
   kebabs 70

mushroom and hazelnut
   pâté 21
mushrooms, stuffed 52
mussels
   mussels vinaigrette 67
   roasted pumpkin and
      smoked mussel soup 8
   stuffed mussels 62
noodles with Japanese
   fishcake 60
ntakos 36
nuts
   nut and cheese pepper
      slices 20
   mushroom and hazelnut
      pâté 21
olive salsa 27
olive tapenade, black 32
omelette salad, Chinese
   vegetable and 56
onion and green pepper pie
   48
pan-cooked prawn kebabs 68
pasta
   kreplach 78
   noodles with Japanese
      fishcake 60
   pasta baskets with
      vegetables 41
   rich egg pasta dough 77
   smoked salmon
      timbales 61
   tomato and pasta
      timbales 42
pâté, mushroom and
   hazelnut 21
   salmon 29
pear Gorgonzola salad 54
pie, onion and green pepper
   48
peppers
   crab and red pepper
      tartlets 64
   nut and cheese pepper
      slices 20
   roasted peppers in oil 50
   Spanish salad of frisée 53
   stuffed peppers 43
pork
   empanadas 79
   sweet and sour pork
      won tons 76
potted ham with
   aubergine 75
prawns, Hawaiian coconut 66
prawn kebabs, pan-broiled 68
pumpkin and smoked mussel
   soup, roasted 8
rich egg pasta dough 77
roasted peppers in oil 50
roasted pumpkin and smoked
   mussel soup 8
roasted tomato tartlets 34
rye crescent rolls 15
salad, Chinese vegetable and
   omelette 56
   pear Gorgonzola 54
   Spanish salad of frisée 53
salmon pâté 29
salmon timbales, smoked 61
salsa, Andalusian 30
   avocado 26
   olive 27
   pineapple 39
sandwich, Cretan 36
seafood chowder 12
smoked salmon timbales 61
soup, crab and sweetcorn 18

Lebanese couscous 16
   roasted pumpkin and
      smoked mussel 8
   seafood chowder 12
   Thai spiced chicken 17
   tomato-basil 13
Spanish salad of frisée 53
spring rolls 55
stuffed mushrooms 52
stuffed mussels 62
stuffed peppers 43
sweet and sour dipping
   sauce 77
sweet and sour pork
   won tons 76
swordfish kebabs, Middle
   Eastern 70
taramasalata 28
tartlets, crab and red
   pepper 64
   roasted tomato 34
Thai lettuce parcels 72
Thai spiced chicken soup 17
timbales, smoked salmon 61
   tomato and pasta 42
toasts, aubergine 37
tomato
   ntakos 36
   roasted tomato tartlets 34
   tomato-basil soup 13
   tomato and heart of palm
      slices 46
   tomato and pasta
      timbales 42
tortilla chips, homemade 31
tortilla wheels with pineapple
   salsa 39
traditional guacamole 23
tuna and aubergine kebabs
   63